Making M&E Work in Development Programmes

A Practitioner's Handbook

DENIKA BLACKLOCK

Lulu Publishing Services rev. date: 02/08/2019

Contents

Introduction: Operationalising M&E Frameworks

Some may feel that this book is bold – bold in that it purports to be yet another handbook on how to develop a results-based monitoring and evaluation (M&E) framework for development programmes. The truth is that this book actually *is* bold – it aims to fill a rather large gap which continues to persist a decade after results-based management gained a strong footing among development organisations both large and small, across the spectrum of issues which constitute development in the 21ˢᵗ century.

What is that gap? It is the cavern between what every M&E handbook tells you *what you should do*, and *actually getting it done*. This book aims to provide guidance on how to operationalise an M&E framework – putting ideas into practice. Ground breaking? No. Useful? Every organisation I have worked or consulted for over the past 10 years tells me absolutely, yes.

So, let us begin. At the beginning. Where we understand how to walk the talk and give legs to the concept of 'results-based M&E'.

Who remembers when 'good' M&E was a simple process of a short narrative section in a project proposal, with a rather sad amount of money for a broad process of 'M&E' in the project budget? When reporting to donors was a simply a process of writing a narrative description of the activities that had been implemented to date – an accounting, if you will, of where the money went – but short on analysis or how the results of activities were being tracked, or even how effective they were. When the number of people trained or the number of micro-grants released was all that really mattered, and we didn't look too far past what would happen at the end of the project. When pre- and post-training tests constituted good monitoring, and we didn't apply ourselves to find out what the micro-grants achieved beyond undertaking a few anecdotal interviews with individuals who were quite obviously successful in their endeavours, failing to uncover why others were not. Gender and social inclusion were certainly not mainstreamed beyond a short paragraph on ensuring that women were involved in activities, but not necessarily recounting in what capacity. Ah, the days when monitoring was a process of financial accountability and not much else.

Fortunately, those days, for the most part, are behind us. With the advent of results-based management (RBM) in development, so too did the idea that M&E should be results-based (eventually) get traction. Handbook after handbook was produced to guide the practitioners among us on what that was supposed to mean. Specifically, 'SMART' indicators, objective baselines, targets that went beyond '# of'.

In practice, the challenge wasn't so much the effort that was needed to ensure that indicators were SMART or that those indicators needed baselines in order to gauge progress against them. No, the challenge in those early days was agreeing on what a *result* was. 'But training people is a result' was the argument over and over from colleagues. It turned out that implementing results-based M&E was more a process of changing mind-sets than it was technical. Making M&E gender-sensitive and socially-inclusive was a pipe dream at that point.

Why was this? People didn't like the idea that they were being asked to do more work (to their minds) when all they wanted to do was get on with implementing activities. Ticking boxes to demonstrate accountability and progress against work plans. No one had ever questioned whether these activities actually created change, and certainly no one worried about how to measure whether change was effected – that was the job of evaluation consultants. Consultants who, now that I am one of them, had to spend precious time developing proxy indicators to better understand what, if any, change had been effected by the activities of a project, and to make an educated guess (based on an understanding of context and capacity) about whether those changes would stick. More than 10 years after results-based M&E was introduced, proxy indicators are still a necessity as far too many projects and programmes have failed to put in place an M&E framework that measures change – in effect, that measures the actual results of a project, not just the input.

So, what is a result? Despite the best efforts of some practitioners to define what a 'result' is, results vary by organisation, by project, and by objective. They are defined by mandates and goals. They can be both quantitative (everyone's favourite) or qualitative (disliked by most but by far more meaningful in development programming). The most important thing to know about 'results' is that they are more than the sum of their parts: they are what you get when you analyse your inputs to a project together with monitoring data and information about context. For example, a result is not how many people were trained, but rather the % of people who were trained and are now using the information/knowledge that they gained to improve the effectiveness of their daily work. We need to be able to determine if the application of that information/knowledge actually made a difference (good/bad). While some might argue this is the definition of an impact, it is important to differentiate between change in the short and medium terms (results) and change over a longer period (impact). Most important of all, it is important to remember that neither development nor M&E are a science and should not be treated as such.

Why, exactly, is M&E so important? For far too long, gathering anecdotal evidence has taken the place of good monitoring. Anecdotal evidence does serve a purpose in the M&E cycle – it provides insights for further exploration and examination, can shed light on issues for project managers to address, supports accountability processes, identifies possible unintended results (good or bad), and provides nice stories for communication and resource mobilisation purposes. But it is not verifiable evidence. Anecdotes from one government department, the token female participant in a village meeting, or two or three households in a village do not evidence make. The ability to claim positive results, change, or even impact rely solely on the collection of good, reliable data through sound methodologies (we'll get to that later). This process needs to be planned well, with serious commitment to implementation as part of the entire project cycle (which I describe how to do below), and is motivated by five objectives[1]:

1. To learn how change happens, as well as what strategies and interventions worked and did not, in order to refine our policies, strategies, and interventions for more effective and impactful change
2. To analyse our role in the change process (to attribute credit or identify cause-effect relationships)
3. To empower our constituencies and ensure social responsibility – to engage stakeholders in analysing change processes so that they are also empowered and strengthened to sustain, extend and expand change
4. To practice accountability and build credibility – to donors, constituencies, other activists and the public at large, and to build legitimacy, credibility and transparency
5. To advance advocacy – to demonstrate how change has advanced our goals and mobilise broader support for the project's agenda

---

Understanding Change versus Impact

Change effected is what results after we have implemented a series of activities to address a specific issue or problem. For example: lack of transparency in government procurement processes leads to many allegations of corruption. With targeted support to improve the procurement system, the qualifications and capacities of procurement personnel and awareness among the community of the government procurement process, we are seeing more transparent procurement, faster procurement and fewer allegations of corruption.

More transparent government procurement and reductions in levels of corruption is the change.

The impact is what happens over the longer term because of that change: improved trust in government, improved publicly procured services and service delivery.

The sixth, and perhaps defining objective of M&E, if we are honest, is that donors require it; your project needs more funding or needs to demonstrate

---

[1] Inspired by 'Capturing Change in Women's Realities' AWID 2010.

how successful the particular approaches or interventions have been. This does not, however, override the importance of the five preceding objectives.

With all of this in mind, who should do M&E? Despite my personal belief that M&E is the responsibility of every member of a project team, not everyone should (time) and not everyone can (technical capacity). But at the very minimum, everyone in a project team should understand why we need a commitment to M&E and provide the necessary support to those responsible for collecting data, analysing it, and drafting reports when they ask for it. Whinging and moaning only causes problems down the road, and begs the question of why it's such a pain for you, the reticent team member, to have to provide a small amount of data that will inevitably make your job easier in the longer term? For example:

- The more regular and rigorous the monitoring process, the more likely that problems in implementation will be identified and dealt with before they spiral out of control and cause far bigger problems down the road
- If you physically can't provide the data or information necessary (records were damaged – it happens – or you actually didn't keep proper records of the activities you were responsible for – true story) then it is better to own up and work together to fix that problem than wait for the donors to wander in to evaluate your project, or worse yet, when the audit rolls around. A few uncomfortable days with your colleagues is far preferable to losing your job later on.

So now that we know that the whingers and moaners probably shouldn't be in charge of the M&E tasks in a project team, let's turn to identifying who should do it. Ask any M&E person and they will tell you that M&E was not originally their intended career path. In my 10 years working in the field of M&E as both staff, advisor, and consultant I have found that the best M&E people have the following qualities:

- They are organised and manage their time well
- They have the capacity for critical analysis (or are willing to learn)

- They have high personal standards when it comes to the products they need to deliver
- They understand why monitoring is important and have ideas about how to use the data and analysis which results from monitoring activities.

Vague? Generic? Perhaps, but I have found that when people who are responsible for M&E are lacking in any (or all, sadly) of the above qualities, they simply cannot get the job done. There are those who can fake it 'til they make it, and that's fine too, but that requires a whole other level of commitment and dedication to learning!

This brings us to the objective of this handbook, which is to provide step-by-step guidance to project managers and staff for implementing the steps and components of monitoring, reporting, and evaluation at the project level. It focuses on the log frame approach to project implementation, because despite the many tools available to development organizations, the log frame remains the most used tool and isn't going anywhere anytime soon (sigh). Thus, it provides advisory guidance, tools, and practical examples and introduces the role of the project team in undertaking 'quality assurance.' It also details some of the experiences and challenges which I have faced over the course of my career which have in turn supported my own learning process, and I hope will help to improve your understanding of the benefits of good monitoring and pitfalls where commitment to monitoring is lacking.

1.

Definitions

Let's set the stage by establishing a common understanding of some key terms in the M&E field. While M&E terms vary between organisations, such as the use of output or key deliverable, outcome, objective or goal, what is most important is that everyone is speaking the same langue. For the purposes of this book, I define the following terms:

Monitoring is an ongoing project management activity. It is undertaken on a frequent and regular basis to assess the implementation of activities and progress towards outputs and outcomes for the purposes of measuring effectiveness and efficiency as well as tracking social responsibility. It is also critical to determining whether work is proceeding according to plan and if sudden or unexpected shifts or reversals have occurred that require management responses in the form of small changes in implementation or large adaptive management measures.

Reporting is the process of providing narrative analysis of the progress your project is making against its objectives. Reporting can be both internal and external and focuses on highlighting the evidence of progress based on monitoring data. There are different types of reports: inception (project set-up), progress (either quarterly or semi-annual), annual, or final. They differ from evaluations in that they report on the data that the project team has collected based on project indicators, and not necessarily on OECD DAC criteria.

Evaluation aims to assess the overall change created by an intervention against an explicit set of outcomes. Evaluation involves the systematic collection, triangulation and analysis of data to help discover if, how and why a particular intervention or set of interventions worked or did not. Evaluations are conducted less frequently than monitoring and aim to capture the big picture of impact, and are used for programme, project or policy improvement, knowledge building and learning. They should be structured around the OECD DAC criteria (relevance, efficiency, effectiveness, accountability, and impact) and other criteria including gender and social accountability (ideally, these are mainstreamed into the DAC criteria analysis). Most important: evaluations must be undertaken by someone external to your organisation, normally an independent consultant.

Frameworks are the broad conceptual structures that attempt to pull together a set of ideas about how a project should be tracked and how its effects should be measured or assessed. This includes results frameworks or log frames, monitoring plans, terms of reference for monitoring, and the tools that will be used to ensure that data collection is consistent throughout the life of a project.

Plans differ from results frameworks or log frames in that they are specific to planning out when, how, and who will implement specific monitoring activities. Good plans will also detail the required resources (human, financial, time) for monitoring to be effectively implemented.

A **tool** is a specific assessment or measurement technique or methodology that is used to generate concrete data or evidence about the results of an intervention or change process. Tools can be used to both establish the baseline of a project and then measure than change that is occurring.

2.

The Monitoring and Evaluation Framework

A **monitoring and evaluation framework** is the starting point from which all monitoring, reporting and evaluation for a project should originate. An M&E framework can be project-based or organisation-based, as long as a project-based framework is aligned with the organisation's principles and guidance on M&E.

M&E frameworks do not need to be complex. In my experience, the more complex an M&E framework, the less commitment a project team has for implementing it. However, the key components of an M&E framework should include, at minimum:

– The **purpose** of monitoring, evaluation and reporting. This section should discuss the approach to monitoring within the project (participatory, etc), how the results will be used (learning, project management, reporting to donors), and how the information will be shared (through reports, feedback sessions, project newsletter, etc).
– The **project log frame or results framework**, which details the project's components, outcomes, outputs, and output indicators, baselines and targets, upon which progress towards project outcomes will be assessed. An important lesson that I have learned is that gender and social inclusion indicators need to be mainstreamed at this point, and not be stand-alone tools if they have any hope of being effective tools for both the project team and beneficiaries.

- A **monitoring and reporting plan**, which must be based on the outputs and indicators in the project's log frame or results framework, and details the tools to be used to monitor individual indicators, a schedule for monitoring, indicative resources required as well as the person responsible for monitoring (either project components, individual indicators, or preparing reports)
- The **terms of reference** of the individual(s) responsible for co-ordinating monitoring, reporting and evaluation for the project. While a specific monitoring and reporting officer/assistant may not be required by the project's organigram, ensuring that the duties for monitoring and reporting are appropriately assigned to (appropriate) staff members is necessary to ensure that monitoring and reporting is undertaken in a timely manner.

2.1   *Developing a Project Log Frame/Results Framework*

Project **log frames** have five essential information 'items':

1. The intended project **outcome**(s)
2. The contributing project **outputs**
3. Output **indicators, baselines and targets**
4. **Activities** corresponding to each output
5. Indicative financial, human and logistical **resources** available by output or activity

Often, log frames will include the means of verification for output indicators (essentially, they are the tools you will use to monitor the indicators). However, this information is not explicitly required in the log frame and is more appropriately located in the project's monitoring plan. A good example of a log frame would look like this[2]:

---

[2] Formats may vary from between organisations, but in terms of content, the most critical information is the outcome/goal; outputs/key deliverables; and activities; outcome and output level indicators, baselines and targets, as well as financial resources required.

Outcome	Output(s)	Output Indicators, Baselines and Targets	Activities	Resources Required
1. Local development plans respond to the expressed needs to communities Indicator: % of community respondents satisfied that the local dev't plan responds to their priorities Baseline: 18% (2009) Targets: 22% (2010) 30% (2011) 37% (2012), etc.	1.1 Local development plans are developed using a community driven approach	Indicators: - Existence of a mechanism to facilitate gender-sensitive community-driven development planning - % of community participating in/contributing to the development planning process (by gender/age/ethnic/economic group) Baselines: - Development planning undertaken through a top-down process - Little involvement of the community beyond village elders Targets: 2010: - Mechanism developed based on good practices in community level decision making - 0 2011: - Mechanism approved by local government - 20% of community participating, 30% of whom are women 2012: etc...	1.1.1 Mechanism developed to ensure participation of all community groups in development planning process	$ 10,000
			1.1.2 Local facilitators are trained to implement community meetings to identify and prioritise community needs	$ 5,000
			1.1.3 Meetings are held in all villages, and include representatives of all community-based groups (incl. Women and youth)	$ 35,000

Depending on the mandate of an organisation or size of a project (or of the organisation itself), outcomes, outputs and activities will be presented differently within the log frame. For example:

	Outcome The development planning process is accountable and transparent	
Output Local development plans respond to the expressed needs to communities	**Outcome** Local development plans respond to the expressed needs to communities	
Activity Local development plans are developed using a community driven approach	**Output** Local development plans are developed using a community driven approach	**Outcome** Local development plans are developed using a community driven approach
	Activity Mechanism developed to ensure participation of all community groups in development planning process	**Output** Mechanism developed to ensure participation of all community groups in development planning process
		Activity Policy framework developed to support community-driven development planning

Regardless of which 'level' your project will be implemented at, outcomes and outputs (but not activities!) will require **indicators** by which to determine progress and change effected, as well as **corresponding targets for each indicator** to determine if the output or outcome has been achieved. And, as noted above, in order to know what your project has achieved, you need **baselines** (by indicator) to know where your project is starting from.

Over the many years and the dozens upon dozens of log frames which I have reviewed, there have been a handful of mistakes that I see repeated time and again. One is when indicators, baselines and targets are not aligned. A second common mistake, as I have noted earlier, are indicators which focus on the inputs to the project (what you did, as opposed to what change you effected). The third most common mistake is when indicators are prescriptive rather than descriptive (i.e.: 'increase in' vs 'change in').

The identification of indicators, development of baselines and setting of targets is independent of activity implementation. Indicators, baselines and targets should respond to the output (or outcome) statement, not to the activities implemented. **This is where the concept of 'results-based' comes in.** If you don't get this part right, your monitoring and reporting runs the risk of being input-oriented and unable to capture change effected by your project. More on this below, but for now, this example: measuring the number of trainings implemented will not tell you if the capacity of local government officials has increased. The only thing the number of trainings will tell you is

> *Activities are a means to an end,* whereas *indicators help you to determine what you need to know to know if you have achieved the output.*

that X number of people attended, received a nice lunch, and possibly a per diem! Instead, look at what the training should result in: for example, increased understanding of participatory development planning/improved tools to implement participatory development planning. Thus, the indicator could focus on the number and gender of participants in development planning meetings, and then the % of those participants (by gender and other socio-economic group!) who are actually applying the knowledge or skills that they gained during the training. You could go one step further to explore how the application of the knowledge and skills creates change, or you could leave to that to the evaluation stage. This is up to you.

Step 1: Developing Indicators

Indicators are tools that measure the change and achievements your project is making against specific outputs (or outcomes). They indicate, but do not prescribe (i.e.: do not presuppose the result with the indicator. For example: % *increase* in communities satisfied with government planning process. We cannot know if an increase can be guaranteed. Instead: % *change* in level of satisfaction of communities with government planning process. If the change is a decrease, it is all the more important to find out why). When brainstorming on possible indicators ("what do we need to know?") you should be guided by the following internationally recognised criteria for quality indicators:

1. meaning of indicator is clear
2. data needed to monitor the indicator is readily or easily available
3. efforts to collect the data is within the power of the project management and does not require experts for analysis

4. indicator is sufficiently representative of the total intended result, including assessing the gender-sensitivity and social-inclusion approach of the intervention
5. indicator is tangible and can be observed
6. indicator is difficult to qualify but is so important it should be considered

These are sometimes referred to as "SMART" criteria: **S**pecific, **M**easurable, **A**chievable, **R**elevant, **T**ime-bound

However, a few observations on these points are necessary.

Point 2: data is readily or easily available. Yes, this is important, but even more important is being aware that it is easy – and erroneous – to choose an indicator because it is easy, rather than appropriate. For example, choosing an indicator on how many development projects were funded in community X versus how many of those projects responded to the needs to the most vulnerable in the community. Counting how many projects were funded? Easy. Assessing how many of those funded met the requirements of being responsive to the needs of the most vulnerable? More time consuming and perhaps more complex, but it provides you with accurate information on your project's achievements rather than generic information not specifically related to your project's objectives. See point 4 below.

Point 3: capacity of the individuals tasked with monitoring indicators. Consider the tools that will be required to monitor the indicators – is the capacity of the individual(s) responsible for monitoring sufficient to ensure reliable monitoring results? Can their capacity be improved in the short term? If not, reconsider the indicator (and tools) to be used. Or reconsider the person responsible for monitoring.

Point 4: does the indicator fall within the parametres of 'what do we need to know in order to determine that we are making progress?' If so, then it is representative of the output/outcome. If not, then it is just superfluous data that you are collecting which provides no evidence and is useless to your team. It is also a waste of your time and resources.

As with the identification of project objectives and activities, indicators should, to the extent possible, be developed in consultation with key project stakeholders, so that they have ownership of the process and are more empowered to contribute to ensuring that the intended changes take place.

Moreover, indicators should capture, or be reflective of, context. For example, if you are working in a country where culturally everything is focussed on the household or community, then it does not really make sense to monitor individuals. The results will not be meaningful to the beneficiaries (even if they are meaningful to you). This is part of being socially accountable. The data that you collect needs to be useful at the beneficiary level, otherwise the only thing that results is a nice report on a (virtual) shelf somewhere.

Key mistakes when developing indicators:

Focusing on activities: # of people trained, or # of meetings held

Irrelevance to output: focusing on inputs instead of beneficiary feedback (i.e.: focus on the usefulness of the training from the beneficiaries' point of view)

Not verifiable: relying solely on data that is not quantifiable (i.e.: beneficiary testimonials)

Not representative: data is not disaggregated by gender, age or geographic area.

Targets as indicators: Policy approved by gov't (target) vs. Existence of new gov't policy (indicator)

Developing indicators to monitor change in capacity

In the field of monitoring and evaluation, there is always tensions between the merits and drawbacks of 'numbers' versus 'stories'. Whereas numbers provide empirical, more objective evidence of change in capacity, stories provide context. In the case of monitoring changes in capacity, numbers are much easier (especially when monitoring change in technical capacities (substantive issues), although it is possible to quantify at least some change in functional capacities (processes/systems)). However, it is not quite as straightforward as one or the other. Your indicators will depend upon the types of capacities your project is working to improve and will more likely than not require a mix of both quantitative and qualitative data. There are a few steps which can help you design the most appropriate indicators for your capacity building activities.

Step 1: Determine what you need to monitor: The table below provides an overview of the areas where interventions may take place, and where monitoring (indicators, tools) can focus its efforts. It is evident from the table that monitoring capacity building requires a multi-dimensional approach.

	Enabling Environment	**Organisational Level**	**Individual Level**
Institutional Arrangements	Policy, legal, regulatory frameworks	Strategy, processes and technology	n/a
Leadership	n/a	Merit-based promotion	Leadership training
Knowledge	*Education systems and education policy reform*	organisational learning strategy or programme	Education, vocational training,
Accountability	Monitoring and regulating processes	Decision-making processes	Addressing vested interests

Step 2: Determine the approach(es) you will use: Will you focus on measuring the project's achievement of its own goals and objectives, or will you focus on measuring the capacity of the beneficiary to satisfy its key stakeholders? (A safe bet is a bit of both, so that you are accountable to both beneficiaries AND donors).

Step 3: Determine how far along the results chain you will monitor: For example, at the output level (improved capacity of the beneficiary to carry out certain tasks); at the outcome level (improved capacity of the beneficiary on certain tasks results in X); or (although unlikely for project monitoring) the impact level (the change created by the increase in the beneficiaries' capacity on their own stakeholders/beneficiaries). Your choice will depend on a) your organization's own capacity for monitoring and b) the purpose that the monitoring data will serve.

Improving project effectiveness with gender-sensitive and socially-inclusive monitoring processes

For the most part, most development practitioners feel that providing sex-disaggregated data constitutes gender-mainstreaming in M&E. In fact, sex disaggregated data doesn't guarantee that you are capturing the different effects of your project on women and men and other vulnerable groups. Your indicators need to be formulated to capture information related to the different experiences of your project on men, women and other vulnerable/socio-economic groups. You need to have data that you can analyze to understand how and why your project impacts different groups in different ways (and whether those impacts are positive or negative).

Gender and socially-inclusive indicators monitor aspects of your project related to participation in and benefits of activities on men and women, and how effective your project is at reaching target groups as well as traditionally marginalized groups. They also help you gather evidence which can support your project in overcoming resistance to gender mainstreaming within target stakeholder and beneficiary groups. Gender mainstreaming is often resisted for reasons relating to entrenched societal standards and norms, power relations, practical issues such as who is available for activities and when, and more psychological resistance such as fear of loss or doubts in capacity to change. When gender-sensitive and socially-inclusive monitoring can be used to present evidence about improved efficiencies and effectiveness in both project implementation and achievements, resistance to gender-mainstreaming can be easier to overcome.

Entry points for making output indicators gender-sensitive and socially-inclusive:

- Assessing the relations between men and women, and between socio-economic groups
- Assessing power relations – in the community, in the household
- Assessing the effect of an activity/project on specific ethnic, socio-economic or cultural groups
- Assessing institutional settings – social systems and their values, legislation, religion and how they impact project implementation and the effectiveness of a project in reaching target beneficiary groups

Step 2: Determining Baselines

The baseline should correspond to the output (or outcome) indicator. For example, if the indicator wants to know %, then the baseline should establish the % at the start of the project. This is often done through the situational or needs assessment or with a specific baseline study. However, in many instances, projects do not have the resources available to them to carry out baseline studies, and situational assessments do not always provide the necessary data in the correct form. In this case, the baseline can be established during the first phase of project monitoring.

It is often the case that baseline data collection is put off repeatedly. This is a sad situation. Without baselines, how will you know if you are making progress or even contributing to a *reversal* in progress? It has been known to happen, and mostly in cases where baselines are either weak, incorrect or absent. Knowingly avoiding the collection of proper – and relevant – baseline data can mean big problems at the end of the project if little to no progress has been made (evaluations can provide evidence of this), with backlash in the form of job loss, withdrawal of funding and even a closure of an organisation (in extreme cases). Better to treat baseline data as a safeguard and simply get it done.

Step 3: Setting Targets

Depending on the length of the project, single targets can be set for each indicator for the life of the project, or the targets for each indicator can be annualised. A general rule of thumb is to annualise targets if the project is more than two years duration.

Targets need to correspond to the wording of the indicator, and numerical value set within both the indicator and target. For example:

Indicator: % change in satisfaction
Baseline: 19% satisfied
Target: 23% satisfied (year 1); 27% satisfied (year 2); 35% satisfied (year 3/end of project)

Targets are important because they allow the project management team to plan activities in accordance with the intensity by which the project wants to see change (the closer the project gets to its closing date, the more intensive change you would likely want to see). Depending on the results of monitoring, targets can also be revised to respond to unforeseen challenges (for example, an unscheduled election interrupts the policy and legislative approval process; or a natural disaster or conflict undermines the ability of the project to implement its capacity building activities in the short or medium term). However, the revision of targets should be done in conjunction with stakeholders, and where possible, with donors to ensure full support for any changes to the project.

One of the biggest mistakes I have seen in my years advising and consulting on M&E is that projects tend to set their targets too low. The rationale? Setting a low target that is easily achievable (or even surpassed!) basically guarantees success. For the most part, this little 'trick' is plain to the eye of an experienced evaluator. And to us, it suggests two things: first, you are more interested in ticking the box to say 'target achieved' than ensuring that the money and time invested in the project results in sustainable change. Consider investigating what level/type of target you need in order to achieve a 'tipping point' – the point where the change you effect has greater than average odds of being sustainable in the long term. Projects that don't go far enough tend to have zero impact. For example, if you are working at the policy level, simply setting a target of 'policy approved' does not mean much. Without the next steps (i.e.: strategic plan and budget for policy implementation approved) change won't happen. If it is the case that 'policy approved' is phase 1 of your project, while policy implementation comes in phase 2, be clear so that you are evaluated fairly.

A Note on Innovation

One of the emerging challenges for M&E practitioners is how to use current tools to monitor activities like advocacy and encouraging innovation. While there are complex tracing tools to monitor changes resulting from advocacy activities, activities encouraging innovation in development provide a unique case. The challenge is this:

Log frames prescribe the change we want to see. Outcome and output statements, and the targets we want to achieve, leave little room for 'new' ideas or processes which may emerge. At best, and until organizations move beyond the log frame as the be all and end all of monitoring, anything 'new' that emerges from a project would be considered an 'unintended' outcome but would not necessarily contribute to the overall achievement of your project against your stated targets.

So, what do we do with the depends for 'innovation' in development?

One option is to **deliberately not set targets** for outputs where you want to encourage innovation. If we set targets, we prescribe the result. If we don't, whatever happens is a success from which we can learn (unless nothing actually happens). For those organizations that insist on targets? A commitment to undertake full lessons learned studies on what happened, why and how in order to learn from the new ideas/processes and determine how best to apply them in the future is one option.

Getting approval for this approach requires organization and project leadership willing to 'walk the talk': not only are they happy discussing innovation, but willing to try new approaches to make it happen. Good luck!

Secondly, projects that repeatedly surpass their targets come across as poorly planned. Perhaps in the first year you surpassed your target due to any number of factors. A competent evaluator will look at those factors and determine if they were a one-off or continue to be present. If the latter, then why do targets remain low? Why is a project not capitalising on a changing context to intensify its implementation if it can? If you are deliberately setting targets low in order to look good when you blow past them, I'm afraid it gives the opposite impression, and does not reflect well on either the project team or the organisation.

A good rule of thumb when setting targets is: what do we reasonably think we can achieve? And then add 10%. Push yourselves, reach that tipping point – make (positive) change happen and ensure it sticks. Remember, targets are not about demonstrating what you did, but reflecting what happened *because of what you did*. Result, result, result.

Step 4: Determining Required Resources

I remember the very first project proposal I developed, and I asked what I should do about the budget for M&E. Stunned silence followed by "maybe $1000?" was the extent of the advice I received. No inputs or suggestions on what monitoring might entail, who would do it, how often it would be done. I probably did throw in $1000 in the budget and hoped for the best because a) I wasn't entirely sure what I was doing drafting a proposal anyway and b) I didn't really have any understanding of what M&E was or what it required. I'm not even sure I knew its purpose. Ah, the naivete of being 24 years old, fresh off the dissertation and wallowing in an unpaid internship.

However, it wasn't long before I began to understand that random numbers on a page was insufficient for the actual process of M&E. Many proposals and projects later, long before I was an M&E practitioner, I began to realise that while I was getting better at determining how much an evaluation might cost (read: going rate for a consultant for 15-20 days) I had little understanding of what monitoring might cost. And not just in relation to money. There were the human and time resources that were required as well. More on that later.

For now, let's concern ourselves with what needs to be done at the project planning stage, when important M&E resource allocation decisions need to be made. Your project log frame needs to denote if resources for monitoring and evaluation will be allocated within a single management output or dispersed across all outputs. There is also the option of using both approaches: funds for an M&E officer, quality assurance (see below), and evaluation within the management output, and funds for monitoring of specific outputs within the budget for each output. Regardless of which approach is taken by the project team, it is important to ensure that resources for monitoring are sufficient, otherwise the project runs the risk of undermining the quality and intensity of its monitoring activities.

Calculating the various aspects of resources required for M&E is detailed the M&E Plan section below.

2.2   Designing a Project Monitoring and Evaluation Plan

Monitoring plans are crucial for project management. Without them, monitoring is usually an *ad hoc* process with little leadership, and does not result in information that is timely, appropriate or provides learning opportunities. Further, without a proper monitoring plan, projects face a much higher risk of going off-track, and lack a mechanism through which to resolve such problems.

Monitoring and evaluation plans should be designed at the beginning of a project, once the M&E framework has been completed. Monitoring and reporting plans should be updated on an annual basis to reflect any changes to the project, or beneficiary or donor requirements. In extreme cases, monitoring plans can be updated more frequently if the situation demands it; for example, if monitoring results indicate that the project has gone off track beyond previously set tolerance levels, or if risks to the project are increasing and complex responses to those risks and challenges are required. Monitoring can become more or less intensive over time depending on the situation. The decision to revise or intensify a monitoring plan is the prerogative of the project manager, or the project manger's supervisor depending on how decentralised the decision-making within an organisation is.

The preparation of a monitoring and reporting plan can be broken down into six straightforward steps:

Step 1: Determine the monitoring tools required by your project

Indicators can be monitored using a variety of tools. Knowing which one (or combination of tools) is the most appropriate depends on three factors:

1. **Knowing how the information that is collected will be used**. Does the project need to know the status of new legislation or

policies? Is the focus on the satisfaction of government or of community beneficiaries? Does the indicator focus on quantity or quality?

2. **The capacity of the individuals who will do the monitoring.** Are the responsible persons capable of implementing the different tools required? For example, are they able to design simple field surveys, administer the survey to a sample of respondents and aggregate the data? Are they able to prepare appropriate, targeted questions for key informant interviews and ask the necessary follow-up or clarifying questions as needed? Are they able to determine which documents need to be reviewed for a document review, and take away the most important/relevant information? If the capacity to undertake these tasks is present, then a project should not restrict itself in which monitoring tools it chooses to use, depending on the resources available. If this level of capacity is not present, the project needs to identify which tools the individual can learn to use effectively with reliable results.

3. **The availability of resources to implement the monitoring.** Consider the human resources required to implement the different monitoring tools and compare those to what the project has available (remember one of the key indicator criteria: collecting data should be within the capacity of the project and not require external expertise). Estimate how much time it will take to monitor the indicators – different tools require varying amounts of time, including planning, implementation and follow-up if required. Finally, do not forget about money. How much will monitoring cost the project (beyond the salaries of the project staff)? Surveys will be far more expensive than document reviews, and key informant interviews and surveys may require travel to destinations necessitating field expenses and time away from other tasks. However, do not fall into the trap of choosing the easiest path to monitoring in order to reduce pressure on available resources. Relying too heavily on one or two methods may cause the project to miss out on important beneficiary feedback, or, more critically, end up with data that cannot be verified and thus presents an unreliable picture of the progress and impact of the project.

Based on the above, you can better determine the project's capacity to implement the most appropriate tool(s) for the indicator. The **most common tools** are:

- **Document reviews**. Document reviews are particularly relevant for tracking the policy, legislative or planning processes. They are often, but not always, combined with key informant interviews or expert panels

- **Awareness/attitude surveys and questionnaires**. Surveys and questionnaires are the most efficient and effective way of obtaining reliable feedback from beneficiaries and stakeholders of the project's activities. While other approaches such as individual interviews and testimonials are adequate for purposes such as case studies and communications materials, the information provided cannot be extrapolated to apply to an entire community or specific group within a community. As such, surveys and questionnaires are an efficient way of obtaining the views of women, youth, the elderly, civil society activists, participants of activities and even individuals who did not participate (for comparison purposes). The data will be more reliable and objective and can be quantified – an important aspect of monitoring where the indicator focuses on 'change'.

- **Key informant interviews**. Key informant interviews are particularly useful for a project when data collected through documents reviews or surveys/questionnaires requires follow-up explanations or supplementary information. The interviewee should be a person of sufficient seniority to be able to understand the 'big picture' in which the project is operating, and well versed on the issue or subject upon which the interview will be focuses. While the results of interviews are difficult to quantify, they often provide complimentary qualitative evidence to survey/questionnaire findings.

- **Focus groups**. Focus group discussions (FGDs) are important tools in that they serve a similar purpose to key informant interviews in providing more in-depth explanations for data obtained through surveys and questionnaires. The difference is that FGDs allow for the targeting of specific groups: women, youth, elderly, traditional leaders, etc. Thus, a number of FGDs can be held to allow for the project to better understand the impacts of its interventions on different groups of beneficiaries. FGDs are a good compliment to survey/questionnaire data, but can also be undertaken as standalone monitoring activities, particularly if the project approach is targeting specific groups within society.

Complex Monitoring Tools: Tracing Policy Advocacy

Monitoring the results policy advocacy is more than the # of meetings or workshops held, or the # of reports published. It is definitely more than presence on social media, radio, newspaper or TV. Monitoring the results of policy advocacy is complex and requires significant research and analytical capacity among monitoring (or wider project) staff.

A tracing tool can be applied, and should apply the following method:

Stage	Purpose	Guiding question	Method	Specific Questions
1	Determine what information is being received by the target stakeholder	What data is provided, for which sector and to whom?	What tool(s) will you use to get the information you need?	What specific questions do you need answered?
2	Determine the quality of the data	Is the data you have collected reliable and sufficient?		
3	Determine who (if anyone) uses the information that is provided to them	Is the data being provided/used by the most appropriate person/people?		
4	Determine how the information is being used (if at all)	Is the information being used for policy development or another purpose? At what stage of the process is it used?		
5	How important have your policy advocacy activities been, if at all?	At what point has your advocacy activity influenced policy development and how?		

- **Expert panels**. Expert panels are most commonly used for monitoring at the outcome level, or for high-level policy-oriented projects. Similar to key informant interviews in their approach, where the respondents answer predetermined questions pertaining specifically to the indicator, expert panels bring together known experts in a specific field, be they from academia, civil society, government, media or the private sector. The data gathered through expert panels can provide more specific and often evidence-based opinions on the issue at hand.

Based on the above criteria and tools, the project team should decide on the most appropriate tool or combination of tools to obtain the necessary data on each output and outcome indicator. There is a delicate balance between effective (the tool(s) that will provide the best quality data) and efficient (in terms of the amount of time and resources spent obtaining that data) monitoring. It is the prerogative of the project manager (or organisation) to determine which aspect takes priority. At the end of the day, the main criteria should be 'which tool(s) will demonstrate to us the **results** of our project'.

Step 2: Determine when monitoring needs to take place

The frequency of monitoring depends on the type of indicators to be monitored. Projects do not need to monitor all indicators with the same frequency. Determining how often **output indicators** need to be monitored directly impacts on the resources necessary to monitor them. As a rule of thumb:

- Indicators focussing on **advocacy for or development of policy, legislative or planning processes** do not necessarily need to be monitored more than once, or a maximum of twice, per year. Policy and legislative processes in particular are very slow, and projects should not waste human resources tracking processes where little change is evident in short time frames.
- Indicators focussing on **capacity building/development** should be monitored more frequently, but generally no more than two times per year. The time lag between capacity building activities and tangible change 'on the ground' (i.e.: in government processes) means that monitoring too often will undermine the capacity of the project to obtain information that demonstrates change on a scale that can be tied to the project's interventions.

- Indicators focussing on **community development** can be monitored more frequently, but generally not more than quarterly. Project's want to be able to capture change on the ground and harness lessons, but at the same time efficiently use financial and human resources.
- Indicators that focus on **change in satisfaction** levels among beneficiaries and stakeholders should not be monitored more than once or twice per year – specifically if the monitoring tool used is a survey. The amount of planning and resources necessary to properly implement a survey precludes more frequent monitoring, and furthermore, perceptions are often slow to change – frequent monitoring will not be able to capture gradual changes in satisfaction.

Evaluation of **outcome indicators** should, as a general rule, only be done during the mid-term and final review stages, with sufficient time to follow up and analyse data for inclusion in project annual reports. However, important changes in context or operational environment may necessitate more frequent monitoring at the outcome level in order to ensure the continued relevance of the project.

Step 3: Identify the resources required

Monitoring requires substantial resources. Project managers need to ensure that monitoring activities are properly budgeted in terms of financial resources, human resources and with sufficient time to **plan, implement and follow-up monitoring activities**. Different monitoring tools require different amounts of resources.

- **Financial resources**. Depending on the monitoring tool to be implemented, financial resources will be either minimal (document reviews) or substantial (questionnaires). Ensure that all necessary travel, administrative and miscellaneous costs (for example, drinks or snacks for participants of FGDs) are calculated into the monitoring budget.
- **Human resources**. How many project staff are needed to effectively undertake monitoring? Document reviews, interviews, focus

group discussions and expert panels can often be assigned to a single individual, however more complex activities such as surveys and questionnaires require more staff for implementation. Ensure that staff members responsible for monitoring activities have the necessary back-up to effectively and efficiently implement their activities.

- **Time**. One of the primary reasons why monitoring is viewed as a hassle and results in unreliable or incomplete data is that project teams underestimate the amount of planning required and how much time will be needed to implement monitoring activities. Further, many projects lack specific monitoring plans, with monitoring occurring as an afterthought, undertaken at the last possible moment and lacking the necessary time for reflection and analysis of the resulting data. Ensure that the planning stage allows for the identification of stakeholders and beneficiaries to be interviewed/surveyed, preparation of documentation/questions/surveys, scheduling of meetings and interviews, and travel arrangements (if required). Ensure sufficient time for activity implementation (one day and up to two weeks depending on the monitoring activity to be implemented). Finally, schedule time to follow up on the activities – preparing back to office reports, following-up on gaps in data or questions arising from interviews or meetings, and finalising monitoring reports to ensure that the data is not misplaced.

Step 4: Identify who is responsible for implementing monitoring activities

While the overall responsibility for, and leadership of, project monitoring should rest with the project manager, specific duties can be assigned to a single monitoring officer or other project staff (responsibilities to be included in their job description/terms of reference) in various forms:

- Responsibility for monitoring all indicators under a single output
- Responsibility for planning of monitoring activities and supporting their implementation
- Responsibility for specific field monitoring activities

The division of labour for monitoring activities is the prerogative of the project manager, as long as all activities are covered, and the responsible person has the necessary capacity and support to do the job. In general, the key duties of an M&E officer include:

- Undertake monitoring of project activities, to assess overall project implementation against objectives, outputs and indicators, in line with the M&E plan
- Based on results of monitoring, where necessary, undertake troubleshooting, suggest corrective measures, and provide assistance to project staff
- Work closely with the project manager to synthesize good practices and lessons learned
- Ensure reporting arrangements are in place and are being implemented so that the reporting requirements (internal and external) are met in a timely manner
- Assist in the preparations for and implementation of any project evaluations or impact assessments

The project manager should ensure that sufficient time, resources and personnel are identified for carrying out quality assurance missions (see below). These missions should be included in the monitoring plan.

Step 5: Determine what types of reports are needed, and when

How often does the project need to report back to its stakeholders (and donors)? What inputs are required? The project manager (or individual responsible for monitoring) should prepare a reporting schedule, and, working back from due dates, determine what needs to be submitted by whom, and when, in order for the project to prepare a quality, results oriented report (progress or annual report, including financial report) based on:

- Analysis of field monitoring data, in particular stakeholder feedback

- Activities undertaken by the project which are not necessarily captured in the log frame, such as coalition building, networking, brokering or policy advice/support
- Updated analysis of the operating environment and risks to the project.

Once determined, the planning for, writing of and follow-up on reporting should be assigned to specific individuals within the project, and included in the monitoring and reporting plan.

Step 6: Determine when evaluations will need to be undertaken

As a general rule, development projects are required to implement evaluations undertaken by external parties at the mid-way point of the project and at the close of a project. In some instances, the short life of a project will preclude the necessity for a mid-term evaluation.

Evaluations, like monitoring, need to be properly planned (drafting the Terms of Reference, recruitment of an external evaluator, scheduling of travel and meetings, and collection of documentation), and allocated sufficient budget resources and time for implementation. Often, the management of an evaluation is delegated to a single individual, with oversight and support from the project manager.

Once the project team has assembled all of the information required by the preceding steps, the monitoring and reporting plan can be finalised, such as the one below:

Task		Item/Method		1	2	3	4	5	6	7	8	9	10	11	12	Responsible Person(s)*	Budget
									Month								
Monitoring	Output Indicators																
	1.1	Document review														John	$100
		Key Informant Interviews (4 people)														John	$150
	1.2	Survey (12 communities)														John	$1500
	2.1	Survey (heads of Central Gov't Depts)														Heather	$200
	2.2	Document review														Heather	$100
	2.3	Survey (donors and network partners)														Heather	$200
	3.1	Expert Panel (online)														Amy	$100
		Survey (15 NGOs)														Amy	$1500
Reporting	Country Reports															James	n/a
	Progress Report															Agnes	n/a
	Annual Report															Agnes	n/a
Evaluation	QA Country Missions															Agnes	$7500
	Mid-Term Review															James/ Agnes	$12,000
															Total		$25,850

*Note: Responsible Person(s) should prepare their own work plans in co-ordination with their supervisors, detailing the specific tasks required to plan, implement and follow up monitoring and reporting activities. This should include a detailed budget breakdown of resources (human, financial and time) required.

Key: ▢ Planning   ▢ Implementation   ■ Follow-up

3.

Implementing Project Monitoring and Reporting

Once a project monitoring and reporting plan is in place, the implementation of the plan should form part of the day-to-day work of the project team, following the monitoring and reporting cycle:

There are five key steps in the project monitoring and reporting cycle. Note that it is a cycle and not a linear process – as information is collected, analysed and reported on, changes to a project may need to be made (including adjustments to the monitoring plan), and fed back into the cycle.

Step 1: Planning your activities

Most of the work has already been undertaken by this stage: tools identified, responsibilities assigned, a schedule for monitoring confirmed. Planning in the implementation phase of monitoring now consists of planning for the individual monitoring activities (see above: 3.2 Designing a Project Monitoring and Reporting Plan Step 3: Resources). To recap:

- **Prepare the materials you will need to implement the monitoring activity**. For a document review, this would consist of preparing a simple list of documents to be read, and questions you will ask yourself while reading them. For interviews and survey, prepare your questions and survey forms.

- **Identify the stakeholders.** How many communities will you survey? Are they geographically representative? Identify stakeholders which need to be interviewed. Then schedule meetings or block off days to do the surveys.
- **What is your budget?** The monitoring and reporting plan will tell you your indicative budget, so be sure to not go the over budget unless justified by extenuating circumstances. Include travel, administrative and other miscellaneous costs to ensure all eventualities are covered.
- **Determine if you need further human resources support.** This can include having a car and driver to reach communities, extra staff to assist in completing the surveys with communities or requesting the support of a financial assistant from the project to deal with the more complex monitoring activities and budgets.

Remember: it is better to plan early than leave it to the last minute. Poor planning will result in poor monitoring – leaving you with data which may not be representative, biased, incomplete or not verifiable.

Step 2: Field monitoring

Your planning is complete – it's time to monitor!! Field monitoring serves three purposes:

1. Data collection against your project indicators
2. Identification of new challenges or problems in the project (as well as new opportunities)
3. Tracking of the external and internal risks to your project (see below: quality assurance)

Remember, monitoring is not about collecting data for the sake of it, but an opportunity for critical self-reflection on the intervention at hand. Be inquisitive – ensure that you fully apply the monitoring tools at hand, but do not be afraid to ask follow-up questions, dig a little bit deeper to learn about the undercurrents of the environment in which your project is operating, and record problems in implementation (do not try to hide them!

Small problems have a tendency to snow-ball into larger, more complex and difficult to resolve issues).

Make sure that you have a process through which you can systematically record the data and information you are collecting. This will ensure that it is stored properly, is easily retrievable by other colleagues, and is comparable with other monitoring data over time.

Step 3: Analysis of monitoring data

Once you have gathered together the monitoring data from various sources, analysis should take place for the entire output. Analysis of the data is what transforms data from 'data' into meaningful interpretations of the progress of the project, changes on the ground as a result of the project, and what needs to be done over the coming activity implementation period.

As you work your way through the data that you have collected, as well as information on any changes in the development context, challenges facing the project and new opportunities presenting themselves, ask yourself the following questions:

- Why events/changes appear to have happened or are happening
- To what extent are the events/changes a result of the project's intervention as compared to other factors influencing the development situation (Remember no single project can change the situation/context on the ground on its own)
- What would happen to those targeted by the intervention if they had not in fact been beneficiaries? At this stage, capacities for gender analysis is important for the project team. Whether this comes in the form of a gender specialist, or if this is undertaken by the M&E officer, it is a capacity that needs to be present and fostered.

Your analysis should result in a solid presentation of what the data 'means' in the wider scope of the project.

Step 4: Report writing

Reporting templates will assist you in using the monitoring data and other information collected during field monitoring, as well as presenting the results of your analysis. The reports should not be used to present activities; rather they should discuss the progress and change on the ground as a result of the project. This is why analysing your monitoring data is so critical. Readers are less interested in the many activities your project has implemented than they are the change those activities have created, and the broader impact of the combined results of all project activities.

Reports should also be used to make recommendations based on your analysis of the project's progress and operating environment. This is a key aspect of 'adaptive management' – knowing what needs to be adjusted, when and how, based on the results of monitoring. Key points to be considered when formulating and presenting recommendations for follow-up by the project team include:

- What can be done to improve positive effects/compensate for negative effects (and what will those effects be on target groups and beneficiaries?)
- What actions are required, and by whom? (and who has the authority to implement the action?)
- What is the time frame, and what are the financial and human resource implications?
- What are the political implications?
- Are special approaches (including training or new partnerships) required?
- What monitoring or follow-up is required?

Remember: you are not writing the report for you (you already know what is happening in your project!), you are writing for readers (such as donors, civil society, academia and government counterparts) who are interested to learn about how your project approach (networking, capacity building, advocacy, community development, etc) works on the ground, what its impacts are and what lessons can be taken away *in the development environment in which you are operating.* Context is important, which is why you need to discuss the challenges, risks and opportunities facing your project. It will assist you in explaining your project's contributions and the sustainability of any change effected.

Step 5: Feedback to project planning and management

Once you have finalised your monitoring reports and drafted your donor reports, make sure that issues arising through your monitoring (new challenges and opportunities to the project, problems in implementation, changes in the level of risk to the project) are properly fed back to other project staff and staff based in the field. Together with the project manager, determine the most appropriate course of action to rectify problems, take advantage of new opportunities, or mitigate (to the extent possible) changing or emerging risks to the project (adaptive management through M&E at its finest!). Monitoring of the implementation of these follow-up actions will be undertaken through quality assurance missions.

4.

Quality Assurance

Quality assurance is a specific function carried out by a senior member of the project staff who is not normally part of the monitoring and reporting process, or ideally, by someone at the programmatic level of an organisation. The purpose of quality assurance is to periodically double check monitoring and reporting outputs by bringing 'fresh eyes' to the monitoring and reporting process. The quality assurance process shadows the monitoring, evaluation and reporting cycle, but has a different starting point:

Step 1: Quality assurance of reports

Prior to submitting reports to donors or other stakeholders, there is typically a review process. Reviewers should carefully read the reports by first comparing the analysis with field monitoring reports, to ensure consistency, and then to pick apart the presentation of the analysis: are the interpretations of the data subjective? Does the report provide evidence to back up claims? Is the analysis 'overreaching'? These are all common mistakes in reports, and the purpose of the reviewer is to catch them before the report is circulated more widely. Be critical. Be picky. The stronger the report is, the more positive reaction from readers. Make sure you provide feedback to the report drafters so that they have sufficient time to incorporate them and allow you to review the report a second time before publication.

Step 2: Feedback and Planning

Track the recommendations made in the reports. Make a record of them and discuss how they will be followed-up on by project staff in the field. Ensure that the follow-up activities are within the scope of the project and are acceptable to all stakeholders.

Step 3: Quality assurance monitoring missions

The purpose of quality assurance monitoring is to verify the data presented in the field monitoring reports. If field monitoring is undertaken quarterly, then it is sufficient to undertake quality assurance monitoring semi-annually. If field monitoring is undertaken semi-annually, then annual quality assurance is sufficient. Quality assurance monitoring is independent of regular field monitoring. The key role of the person implementing the quality assurance mission is to double check the data provided in the monitoring reports through key informant interviews and focus group discussions. The mission should also take the opportunity to assess the satisfaction of stakeholders with the project management, ascertain any problems and monitor the risks and issues to the project in the field.

Step 4: Feedback

Quality assurance reports should be prepared and discussed with senior project staff, and feedback provided to the project field staff within 10 working days for their follow-up. Track the implementation of follow-up actions through the next field monitoring reports.

5.

Evaluation

5.1 Purpose of an Evaluation

Evaluation is a process which is undertaken by an independent, external evaluator to assess the overall relevance, effectiveness, efficiency, sustainability and impact of a project. Generally, evaluations will focus on the results and process, rather than the inputs, of a project.

While project evaluations tend to focus on the output level, the evaluation should also take into consideration the 'bigger' picture at the outcome level. In some instances, projects will undertake two separate evaluations: one for relevance, effectiveness, efficiency and sustainability, and another for impact.

Global practice strongly recommends the use of the OECD Development Assistance Committee (DAC) Evaluation Criteria (often known as the 'DAC Criteria'). The DAC Criteria attempts to ensure that evaluations are done in line with international agreements such as the Paris Declaration on aid effectiveness. It is thus important to understand what is meant by relevance, effectiveness, efficiency, sustainability and impact.

Criteria	Evaluation Questions
Relevance: The extent to which the aid activity is suited to the priorities and policies of the target group, recipient and donor.	• To what extent are the objectives of the programme still valid? • Are the activities and outputs of the programme consistent with the overall goal and the attainment of its objectives? • Are the activities and outputs of the programme consistent with the intended impacts and effects?
Effectiveness: A measure of the extent to which an aid activity attains its objectives.	• To what extent were the objectives achieved / are likely to be achieved? • What were the major factors influencing the achievement or non-achievement of the objectives?
Efficiency: Measuring the outputs – using qualitative and quantitative methods -- in relation to the inputs. It is an economic term which signifies that the aid uses the least costly resources possible in order to achieve the desired results. This generally requires comparing alternative approaches to achieving the same outputs, to see whether the most efficient process has been adopted.	• Were activities cost-efficient? • Were objectives achieved on time? • Was the programme or project implemented in the most efficient way compared to alternatives?
Sustainability: Measuring whether the benefits of an activity are likely to continue after donor funding has been withdrawn. Projects need to be environmentally as well as financially sustainable.	• To what extent did the benefits of a programme or project continue after donor funding ceased? • What were the major factors which influenced the achievement or non-achievement of sustainability of the programme or project?
Impact: The positive and negative changes produced by a development intervention, directly or indirectly, intended or unintended. This involves the main impacts and effects resulting from the activity on the local social, economic, environmental and other development indicators. The evaluation should be concerned with both intended and unintended results and must also include the positive and negative impact of external factors, such as changes in terms of trade and financial conditions.	• What has happened as a result of the programme or project? • What real difference has the activity made to the beneficiaries? • How many people have been affected?

Some projects take the opportunity to include evaluation of their substantive approaches within the evaluation framework, such as focusing on capacity development, gender mainstreaming and social inclusion strategies, environmental sustainability and adaptive management capacity.

Evaluations also take advantage of an opportunity to obtain an outsider's perspective of good practices and lessons to take away from the project and apply elsewhere. Note: It is far better to use the term 'good practices' rather than 'best practices' as 'practices' are not always best for every situation, but provide good guidance to other, similar projects either in the region or globally. I find the following to be a useful way to organise lessons learned in an evaluation: what has been done well; what could be done better; what has not worked out and why.

5.2   Designing an Evaluation

Planning for an evaluation is an important part of your M&E plan. Experience demonstrates that effectively implemented evaluations begin planning for them three months prior to their implementation.

Step 1: Prepare the Terms of Reference (TOR) for the external consultant

This should include a short description of the project, the objectives of the evaluation (many TORs simply copy, past and amend slightly the DAC Criteria), expected deliverable (e.g.: inception report, draft report, final report), the schedule, budget (Fees, international and field mission travel, per diems and miscellaneous costs) and required qualifications of the consultant.

Step 2: Recruit the consultant

You can do this through your organisation's roster of consultants or advertise publicly. Consultants should provide a brief overview of their intended approach and the methodology they will use during the evaluation based on information provided in the TOR. They should also be able to provide a standard against which they will rate the project – for example, a scale of 1-5 on quality of management, efficiency, results, likelihood of sustainability, and provide justifications for such ratings.

Step 3: Prepare all necessary background information

Compile a list of documents you want the consultant to review and begin compiling them. Then prepare the list of stakeholders and beneficiaries to be interviewed by the consultant. During the inception phase of the evaluation, the consultant may request further documents for review and list other stakeholders to interview. Ensure that one person from the organisation is assigned to accompany the consultant on the various field missions for logistic and translation (if necessary) purposes.

Step 4: Support the field missions of the consultant

Ensure that the consultant receives the support necessary to carryout field visits, including logistical support, organising follow-up meetings based on the outcomes of other meetings, providing clarifications on data and observations as necessary.

Step 5: Provide feedback on the draft evaluation report

Ensure rapid turn-around on feedback to the consultant's draft report. Make sure project staff know to allot time during a specific number of days to review and comment on the draft report so that the process does not drag on, and the consultant can finalise the evaluation.

Step 6: Implement management responses to evaluation findings

Prepare management responses to the findings and recommendations and schedule any follow-up actions required, including budget revisions and adaptation in project approach as necessary.

Conclusion

M&E is far from the sexiest part of development, but if done correctly, it can be interesting. If you like problem solving, like me, then M&E may well be a very good fit for you. It is my intention that the preceding information assists you in your task of designing an M&E framework that's fit for purpose and keeps your work interesting.

Understanding where monitoring fits at every stage of the project cycle is important and allows monitoring staff to ensure that their knowledge and skills are relevant to project staff every step of the way. Ensuring that project staff know this and know when they can call upon the skills of monitoring staff is critical and makes for more robust project management. Problems can be more easily identified, solutions agreed and implemented in a shorter time frame. Communication between monitoring staff and other project team members needs to be encouraged and fostered.

However, I leave the most important information and advice for last: in order for M&E to work – and work properly – for your project, a strong framework is one of the factors required. The other factor is strong leadership – from project management as well as the organisation. When management commitment on M&E is weak, then M&E is ineffective. Only the most basic of requirements are met, and the process does not benefit the project, the stakeholders, or the beneficiaries. Monitoring to tick a box is irresponsible and not actually monitoring. Monitoring to learn and provide accountability is a much more appropriate way of doing business and improves not only project effectiveness, but efficiency, sustainability and long-term impact, if done well.

In sum, changing mindsets towards M&E will be a big part of your job, if not your job description, whether you are a project manager or a monitoring officer. I hope that this book is helpful to you in providing step-by-step guidance to support the implementation of, and learning about, M&E in your project.

To Fakri, Adam and Ruqayyah
Thanks for letting me be me.

www.ingramcontent.com/pod-product-compliance
Lightning Source LLC
Chambersburg PA
CBHW021931170526
45157CB00005B/2276